P9-CJJ-895

HOWL

AND OTHER POEMS
BY
ALLEN GINSBERG

' Unscrew the locks from the doors !
Unscrew the doors themselves from their jambs !'

CITY LIGHTS BOOKS
San Francisco

© 1956, 1959 by Allen Ginsberg
All Rights Reserved
1,060,000 copies in print

Library of Congress Catalog Card Number: 56-8587

ISBN 10: 0-87286-017-5
ISBN 13: 978-0-87286-017-9

Mixed Sources
Product group from well-managed
forests and other controlled sources
www.fsc.org Cert no. SW-COC-002283
© 1996 Forest Stewardship Council
FSC

Vist our website: www.citylights.com

CITY LIGHTS BOOKS are edited by Lawrence Ferlinghetti and
Nancy J. Peters and published at the City Lights Bookstore, 261
Columbus Avenue, San Francisco, CA 94133.

DEDICATION

To—

Jack Kerouac, new Buddha of American prose, who spit forth intelligence into eleven books written in half the number of years (1951-1956)—*On the Road, Visions of Neal, Dr. Sax, Springtime Mary, The Subterraneans, San Francisco Blues, Some of the Dharma, Book of Dreams, Wake Up, Mexico City Blues,* and *Visions of Gerard*—creating a spontaneous bop prosody and original classic literature. Several phrases and the title of *Howl* are taken from him.

William Seward Burroughs, author of *Naked Lunch,* an endless novel which will drive everybody mad.

Neal Cassady, author of *The First Third,* an autobiography (1949) which enlightened Buddha.

All these books are published in Heaven.

CONTENTS

HOWL FOR CARL SOLOMON

When he was younger, and I was younger, I used to know Allen Ginsberg, a young poet living in Paterson, New Jersey, where he, son of a well-known poet, had been born and grew up. He was physically slight of build and mentally much disturbed by the life which he had encountered about him during those first years after the First World War as it was exhibited to him in and about New York City. He was always on the point of 'going away', where it didn't seem to matter; he disturbed me, I never thought he'd live to grow up and write a book of poems. His ability to survive, travel, and go on writing astonishes me. That he has gone on developing and perfecting his art is no less amazing to me.

Now he turns up fifteen or twenty years later with an arresting poem. Literally he has, from all the evidence, been through hell. On the way he met a man named Carl Solomon with whom he shared among the teeth and excrement of this life something that cannot be described but in the words he has used to describe it. It is a howl of defeat. Not defeat at all for he has gone through defeat as if it were an ordinary experience, a trivial experience. Everyone in this life is defeated but a man, if he be a man, is not defeated.

It is the poet, Allen Ginsberg, who has gone, in his own body, through the horrifying experiences described from life in these pages. The wonder of the thing is not that he has survived but that he, from the very depths, has found a fellow whom he can love, a love he celebrates without looking aside in these poems. Say what you will, he proves to us, in spite of the most debasing experiences that life can offer a man, the spirit of love survives to ennoble our lives if we have the wit and the courage and the faith—and the art! to persist.

It is the belief in the art of poetry that has gone hand in hand with this man into his Golgotha, from that charnel house, similar in every way, to that of the Jews in the past war. But this is in our own country, our own fondest purlieus. We are blind and live our blind lives out in blindness. Poets are damned but they are not blind, they see with the eyes of the angels. This poet sees through and all around the horrors he partakes of in the very intimate details of his poem. He avoids nothing but experiences it to the hilt. He contains it. Claims it as his own—and, we believe, laughs at it and has the time and affrontery to love a fellow of his choice and record that love in a well-made poem.

Hold back the edges of your gowns, Ladies, we are going through hell.

William Carlos Williams

HOWL

For
Carl Solomon

helped ignite counterculture and unite the Beatniks throughout the country

I

I saw the best minds of my generation destroyed by
madness, starving hysterical naked,

dragging themselves through the negro streets at dawn
looking for an angry fix,

angelheaded hipsters burning for the ancient heavenly
connection to the starry dynamo in the machinery of night,

who poverty and tatters and hollow-eyed and high sat
up smoking in the supernatural darkness of
cold-water flats floating across the tops of cities
contemplating jazz,

who bared their brains to Heaven under the El and
saw Mohammedan angels staggering on tenement roofs illuminated,

who passed through universities with radiant cool eyes
hallucinating Arkansas and Blake-light tragedy
among the scholars of war,

who were expelled from the academies for crazy &
publishing obscene odes on the windows of the
skull,

the Beats were intelligent, informed, despite what people assumed

who cowered in unshaven rooms in underwear, burning their money in wastebaskets and listening
to the Terror through the wall,
who got busted in their pubic beards returning through
Laredo with a belt of marijuana for New York,
who ate fire in paint hotels or drank turpentine in
Paradise Alley, death, or purgatoried their
torsos night after night
with dreams, with drugs, with waking nightmares, al-
cohol and cock and endless balls,
incomparable blind streets of shuddering cloud and
lightning in the mind leaping toward poles of
Canada & Paterson, illuminating all the mo-
tionless world of Time between,
Peyote solidities of halls, backyard green tree cemetery
dawns, wine drunkenness over the rooftops,
storefront boroughs of teahead joyride neon
blinking traffic light, sun and moon and tree
vibrations in the roaring winter dusks of Brooklyn, ashcan rantings and kind king light of mind,
who chained themselves to subways for the endless
ride from Battery to holy Bronx on benzedrine
until the noise of wheels and children brought
them down shuddering mouth-wracked and
battered bleak of brain all drained of brilliance
in the drear light of Zoo,

who sank all night in submarine light of Bickford's
    floated out and sat through the stale beer after-
    noon in desolate Fugazzi's, listening to the crack
    of doom on the hydrogen jukebox,
who talked continuously seventy hours from park to
    pad to bar to Bellevue to museum to the Brook-
    lyn Bridge,
a lost battalion of platonic conversationalists jumping
    down the stoops off fire escapes off windowsills
    off Empire State out of the moon,
yacketayakking screaming vomiting whispering facts
    and memories and anecdotes and eyeball kicks
    and shocks of hospitals and jails and wars,
whole intellects disgorged in total recall for seven days
    and nights with brilliant eyes, meat for the
    Synagogue cast on the pavement,
who vanished into nowhere Zen New Jersey leaving a
    trail of ambiguous picture postcards of Atlantic
    City Hall,
suffering Eastern sweats and Tangerian bone-grind-
    ings and migraines of China under junk-with-
    drawal in Newark's bleak furnished room,
who wandered around and around at midnight in the
    railroad yard wondering where to go, and went,
    leaving no broken hearts,

who lit cigarettes in boxcars boxcars boxcars racketing
      through snow toward lonesome farms in grand-
      father night,

who studied Plotinus Poe St. John of the Cross telep-
      athy and bop kabbalah because the cosmos in-
      stinctively vibrated at their feet in Kansas,

who loned it through the streets of Idaho seeking vis-
      ionary indian angels who were visionary indian
      angels,

who thought they were only mad when Baltimore
      gleamed in supernatural ecstasy,

who jumped in limousines with the Chinaman of Okla-
      homa on the impulse of winter midnight street-
      light smalltown rain,

who lounged hungry and lonesome through Houston
      seeking jazz or sex or soup, and followed the
      brilliant Spaniard to converse about America
      and Eternity, a hopeless task, and so took ship
      to Africa,

who disappeared into the volcanoes of Mexico leaving
      behind nothing but the shadow of dungarees
      and the lava and ash of poetry scattered in fire-
      place Chicago,

who reappeared on the West Coast investigating the
      F.B.I. in beards and shorts with big pacifist
      eyes sexy in their dark skin passing out incom-
      prehensible leaflets,

who burned cigarette holes in their arms protesting
    the narcotic tobacco haze of Capitalism,
who distributed Supercommunist pamphlets in Union
    Square weeping and undressing while the sirens
    of Los Alamos wailed them down, and wailed
    down Wall, and the Staten Island ferry also
    wailed,
who broke down crying in white gymnasiums naked
    and trembling before the machinery of other
    skeletons,
who bit detectives in the neck and shrieked with delight
    in policecars for committing no crime but their
    own wild cooking pederasty and intoxication,
who howled on their knees in the subway and were
    dragged off the roof waving genitals and manu-
    scripts,
who let themselves be fucked in the ass by saintly
    motorcyclists, and screamed with joy,
who blew and were blown by those human seraphim,
    the sailors, caresses of Atlantic and Caribbean
    love,
who balled in the morning in the evenings in rose-
    gardens and the grass of public parks and
    cemeteries scattering their semen freely to
    whomever come who may,

who hiccuped endlessly trying to giggle but wound up
with a sob behind a partition in a Turkish Bath
when the blond & naked angel came to pierce
them with a sword,

who lost their loveboys to the three old shrews of fate
the one eyed shrew of the heterosexual dollar
the one eyed shrew that winks out of the womb
and the one eyed shrew that does nothing but
sit on her ass and snip the intellectual golden
threads of the craftsman's loom,

who copulated ecstatic and insatiate with a bottle of
beer a sweetheart a package of cigarettes a can-
dle and fell off the bed, and continued along
the floor and down the hall and ended fainting
on the wall with a vision of ultimate cunt and
come eluding the last gyzym of consciousness,

who sweetened the snatches of a million girls trembling
in the sunset, and were red eyed in the morning
but prepared to sweeten the snatch of the sunrise, flashing buttocks under barns and naked
in the lake,

who went out whoring through Colorado in myriad
stolen night-cars, N.C., secret hero of these
poems, cocksman and Adonis of Denver—joy
to the memory of his innumerable lays of girls
in empty lots & diner backyards, moviehouses'

rickety rows, on mountaintops in caves or with
gaunt waitresses in familiar roadside lonely pet-
ticoat upliftings & especially secret gas-station
solipsisms of johns, & hometown alleys too,

who faded out in vast sordid movies, were shifted in
dreams, woke on a sudden Manhattan, and
picked themselves up out of basements hung-
over with heartless Tokay and horrors of Third
Avenue iron dreams & stumbled to unemploy-
ment offices,

who walked all night with their shoes full of blood on
the snowbank docks waiting for a door in the
East River to open to a room full of steamheat
and opium,

who created great suicidal dramas on the apartment
cliff-banks of the Hudson under the wartime
blue floodlight of the moon & their heads shall
be crowned with laurel in oblivion,

who ate the lamb stew of the imagination or digested
the crab at the muddy bottom of the rivers of
Bowery,

who wept at the romance of the streets with their
pushcarts full of onions and bad music,

who sat in boxes breathing in the darkness under the
bridge, and rose up to build harpsichords in
their lofts,

who coughed on the sixth floor of Harlem crowned
with flame under the tubercular sky surrounded
by orange crates of theology,

who scribbled all night rocking and rolling over lofty
incantations which in the yellow morning were
stanzas of gibberish,

who cooked rotten animals lung heart feet tail borsht
& tortillas dreaming of the pure vegetable
kingdom,

who plunged themselves under meat trucks looking for
an egg,

who threw their watches off the roof to cast their ballot
for Eternity outside of Time, & alarm clocks
fell on their heads every day for the next decade,

who cut their wrists three times successively unsuccess-
fully, gave up and were forced to open antique
stores where they thought they were growing
old and cried,

who were burned alive in their innocent flannel suits
on Madison Avenue amid blasts of leaden verse
& the tanked-up clatter of the iron regiments
of fashion & the nitroglycerine shrieks of the
fairies of advertising & the mustard gas of sinister intelligent editors, or were run down by the
drunken taxicabs of Absolute Reality,

who jumped off the Brooklyn Bridge this actually hap-
    pened and walked away unknown and forgotten
    into the ghostly daze of Chinatown soup alley-
    ways & firetrucks, not even one free beer,
who sang out of their windows in despair, fell out of
    the subway window, jumped in the filthy Pas-
    saic, leaped on negroes, cried all over the street,
    danced on broken wineglasses barefoot smashed
    phonograph records of nostalgic European
    1930s German jazz finished the whiskey and
    threw up groaning into the bloody toilet, moans
    in their ears and the blast of colossal steam-
    whistles,
who barreled down the highways of the past journeying
    to each other's hotrod-Golgotha jail-solitude
    watch or Birmingham jazz incarnation,
who drove crosscountry seventytwo hours to find out
    if I had a vision or you had a vision or he had
    a vision to find out Eternity,
who journeyed to Denver, who died in Denver, who
    came back to Denver & waited in vain, who
    watched over Denver & brooded & loned in
    Denver and finally went away to find out the
    Time, & now Denver is lonesome for her heroes,

who fell on their knees in hopeless cathedrals praying
for each other's salvation and light and breasts,
until the soul illuminated its hair for a second,

who crashed through their minds in jail waiting for
impossible criminals with golden heads and the
charm of reality in their hearts who sang sweet
blues to Alcatraz,

who retired to Mexico to cultivate a habit, or Rocky
Mount to tender Buddha or Tangiers to boys
or Southern Pacific to the black locomotive or
Harvard to Narcissus to Woodlawn to the
daisychain or grave,

who demanded sanity trials accusing the radio of hyp-
notism & were left with their insanity & their
hands & a hung jury,

who threw potato salad at CCNY lecturers on Dadaism
and subsequently presented themselves on the
granite steps of the madhouse with shaven heads
and harlequin speech of suicide, demanding in-
stantaneous lobotomy,

and who were given instead the concrete void of insulin
Metrazol electricity hydrotherapy psycho-
therapy occupational therapy pingpong &
amnesia,

who in humorless protest overturned only one symbolic
pingpong table, resting briefly in catatonia,

returning years later truly bald except for a wig of
blood, and tears and fingers, to the visible madman doom of the wards of the madtowns of the
East,

Pilgrim State's Rockland's and Greystone's foetid
halls, bickering with the echoes of the soul, rocking and rolling in the midnight solitude-bench
dolmen-realms of love, dream of life a nightmare, bodies turned to stone as heavy as the
moon, *why the omission?*

with mother finally ******, and the last fantastic book
flung out of the tenement window, and the last
door closed at 4 A.M. and the last telephone
slammed at the wall in reply and the last fur-
nished room emptied down to the last piece of
mental furniture, a yellow paper rose twisted
on a wire hanger in the closet, and even that
imaginary, nothing but a hopeful little bit of
hallucination—

1st time he really addressed Carl, and ties Carl aside

ah, Carl, while you are not safe I am not safe, and
now you're really in the total animal soup of
time—

and who therefore ran through the icy streets obsessed
with a sudden flash of the alchemy of the use
of the ellipse the catalog the meter & the vibrat-
ing plane,

who dreamt and made incarnate gaps in Time & Space
through images juxtaposed, and trapped the
archangel of the soul between 2 visual images
and joined the elemental verbs and set the noun
and dash of consciousness together jumping
with sensation of Pater Omnipotens Aeterna
Deus

to recreate the syntax and measure of poor human
prose and stand before you speechless and intelligent and shaking with shame, rejected yet con-
fessing out the soul to conform to the rhythm
of thought in his naked and endless head,

the madman bum and angel beat in Time, unknown,
yet putting down here what might be left to say
in time come after death,

and rose reincarnate in the ghostly clothes of jazz in
the goldhorn shadow of the band and blew the
suffering of America's naked mind for love into
an eli eli lamma lamma sabacthani saxophone
cry that shivered the cities down to the last radio

with the absolute heart of the poem of life butchered
out of their own bodies good to eat a thousand
years.

II

What sphinx of cement and aluminum bashed open
their skulls and ate up their brains and imagination?

Moloch! Solitude! Filth! Ugliness! Ashcans and unob-
tainable dollars! Children screaming under the
stairways! Boys sobbing in armies! Old men
weeping in the parks!

Moloch! Moloch! Nightmare of Moloch! Moloch the
loveless! Mental Moloch! Moloch the heavy
judger of men!

Moloch the incomprehensible prison! Moloch the
crossbone soulless jailhouse and Congress of
sorrows! Moloch whose buildings are judgment!
Moloch the vast stone of war! Moloch the stun-
ned governments!

Moloch whose mind is pure machinery! Moloch whose
blood is running money! Moloch whose fingers
are ten armies! Moloch whose breast is a canni-
bal dynamo! Moloch whose ear is a smoking
tomb!

Moloch whose eyes are a thousand blind windows!
Moloch whose skyscrapers stand in the long
streets like endless Jehovahs! Moloch whose factories dream and croak in the fog! Moloch whose
smokestacks and antennae crown the cities!

Moloch whose love is endless oil and stone! Moloch
whose soul is electricity and banks! Moloch
whose poverty is the specter of genius! Moloch
whose fate is a cloud of sexless hydrogen!
Moloch whose name is the Mind!

Moloch in whom I sit lonely! Moloch in whom I dream
Angels! Crazy in Moloch! Cocksucker in
Moloch! Lacklove and manless in Moloch!

Moloch who entered my soul early! Moloch in whom
I am a consciousness without a body! Moloch
who frightened me out of my natural ecstasy!
Moloch whom I abandon! Wake up in Moloch!
Light streaming out of the sky!

Moloch! Moloch! Robot apartments! invisible suburbs!
skeleton treasuries! blind capitals! demonic
industries! spectral nations! invincible mad
houses! granite cocks! monstrous bombs!

They broke their backs lifting Moloch to Heaven! Pavements, trees, radios, tons! lifting the city to
Heaven which exists and is everywhere about
us!

Visions! omens! hallucinations! miracles! ecstasies!
gone down the American river!

Dreams! adorations! illuminations! religions! the whole
boatload of sensitive bullshit!

Breakthroughs! over the river! flips and crucifixions!
gone down the flood! Highs! Epiphanies! De-
spairs! Ten years' animal screams and suicides!
Minds! New loves! Mad generation! down on
the rocks of Time!

Real holy laughter in the river! They saw it all! the
wild eyes! the holy yells! They bade farewell!
They jumped off the roof! to solitude! waving!
carrying flowers! Down to the river! into the
street!

moves to an affirmation

III

Carl Solomon! I'm with you in Rockland
      where you're madder than I am

similar to Whitman

I'm with you in Rockland
      where you must feel very strange
I'm with you in Rockland
      where you imitate the shade of my mother
I'm with you in Rockland
      where you've murdered your twelve secretaries
I'm with you in Rockland
      where you laugh at this invisible humor
I'm with you in Rockland
      where we are great writers on the same dreadful
      typewriter
I'm with you in Rockland

mental illness or the "condition" of homosexuality?

      where your condition has become serious and
      is reported on the radio
I'm with you in Rockland
      where the faculties of the skull no longer admit
      the worms of the senses
I'm with you in Rockland
      where you drink the tea of the breasts of the
      spinsters of Utica
I'm with you in Rockland
      where you pun on the bodies of your nurses the
      harpies of the Bronx

I'm with you in Rockland
>   where you scream in a straightjacket that you're
>   losing the game of the actual pingpong of the
>   abyss

I'm with you in Rockland
>   where you bang on the catatonic piano the soul
>   is innocent and immortal it should never die
>   ungodly in an armed madhouse

I'm with you in Rockland
>   where fifty more shocks will never return your
>   soul to its body again from its pilgrimage to a
>   cross in the void

I'm with you in Rockland
>   where you accuse your doctors of insanity and
>   plot the Hebrew socialist revolution against the
>   fascist national Golgotha

I'm with you in Rockland
>   where you will split the heavens of Long Island
>   and resurrect your living human Jesus from the
>   superhuman tomb

I'm with you in Rockland
>   where there are twenty-five-thousand mad com-
>   rades all together singing the final stanzas of
>   the Internationale

I'm with you in Rockland
>where we hug and kiss the United States under
>our bedsheets the United States that coughs all
>night and won't let us sleep

I'm with you in Rockland
>where we wake up electrified out of the coma
>by our own souls' airplanes roaring over the
>roof they've come to drop angelic bombs the
>hospital illuminates itself   imaginary walls col-
>lapse   O skinny legions run outside   O starry-
>spangled shock of mercy the eternal war is
>here   O victory forget your underwear we're
>free

I'm with you in Rockland
>in my dreams you walk dripping from a sea-
>journey on the highway across America in tears
>to the door of my cottage in the Western night

San Francisco 1955-56

FOOTNOTE TO HOWL

Holy! Holy! Holy! Holy! Holy! Holy! Holy! Holy! Holy!
Holy! Holy! Holy! Holy! Holy! Holy!

The world is holy! The soul is holy! The skin is holy!
The nose is holy! The tongue and cock and hand
and asshole holy!

Everything is holy! everybody's holy! everywhere is
holy! everyday is in eternity! Everyman's an
angel!

The bum's as holy as the seraphim! the madman is
holy as you my soul are holy!

The typewriter is holy the poem is holy the voice is
holy the hearers are holy the ecstasy is holy!

Holy Peter holy Allen holy Solomon holy Lucien holy
Kerouac holy Huncke holy Burroughs holy Cassady holy the unknown buggered and suffering
beggars holy the hideous human angels!

Holy my mother in the insane asylum! Holy the cocks
of the grandfathers of Kansas!

Holy the groaning saxophone! Holy the bop
apocalypse! Holy the jazzbands marijuana
hipsters peace & junk & drums!

Holy the solitudes of skyscrapers and pavements! Holy
the cafeterias filled with the millions! Holy the
mysterious rivers of tears under the streets!

resulting transformation from alienation to beatific love

Holy the lone juggernaut! Holy the vast lamb of the
    middle class! Holy the crazy shepherds of rebell-
    ion! Who digs Los Angeles IS Los Angeles!

Holy New York Holy San Francisco Holy Peoria &
    Seattle Holy Paris Holy Tangiers Holy Moscow
    Holy Istanbul!

Holy time in eternity holy eternity in time holy the
    clocks in space holy the fourth dimension holy
    the fifth International holy the Angel in Moloch!

Holy the sea holy the desert holy the railroad holy the
    locomotive holy the visions holy the hallucina-
    tions holy the miracles holy the eyeball holy the
    abyss!

Holy forgiveness! mercy! charity! faith! Holy! Ours!
    bodies! suffering! magnanimity!

Holy the supernatural extra brilliant intelligent
    kindness of the soul!

Berkeley, 1955

A SUPERMARKET IN CALIFORNIA

What thoughts I have of you tonight, Walt Whitman, for I walked down the sidestreets under the trees with a headache self-conscious looking at the full moon.

In my hungry fatigue, and shopping for images, I went into the neon fruit supermarket, dreaming of your enumerations!

What peaches and what penumbras! Whole families shopping at night! Aisles full of husbands! Wives in the avocados, babies in the tomatoes!—and you, García Lorca, what were you doing down by the watermelons?

I saw you, Walt Whitman, childless, lonely old grubber, poking among the meats in the refrigerator and eyeing the grocery boys.

I heard you asking questions of each: Who killed the pork chops? What price bananas? Are you my Angel?

I wandered in and out of the brilliant stacks of cans following you, and followed in my imagination by the store detective.

We strode down the open corridors together in our solitary fancy tasting artichokes, possessing every frozen delicacy, and never passing the cashier.

Where are we going, Walt Whitman? The doors close in an hour. Which way does your beard point tonight?

(I touch your book and dream of our odyssey in the supermarket and feel absurd.)

Will we walk all night through solitary streets? The trees add shade to shade, lights out in the houses, we'll both be lonely.

Will we stroll dreaming of the lost America of love past blue automobiles in driveways, home to our silent cottage?

Ah, dear father, graybeard, lonely old courage-teacher, what America did you have when Charon quit poling his ferry and you got out on a smoking bank and stood watching the boat disappear on the black waters of Lethe?

Berkeley 1955

TRANSCRIPTION OF ORGAN MUSIC

The flower in the glass peanut bottle formerly in the
      kitchen crooked to take a place in the light,
the closet door opened, because I used it before, it
      kindly stayed open waiting for me, its owner.

I began to feel my misery in pallet on floor, listening
      to music, my misery, that's why I want to sing.
The room closed down on me, I expected the presence
      of the Creator, I saw my gray painted walls and
      ceiling, they contained my room, they contained
      me
as the sky contained my garden,
I opened my door

      The rambler vine climbed up the cottage post,
the leaves in the night still where the day had placed
them, the animal heads of the flowers where they had
arisen
      to think at the sun

      Can I bring back the words? Will thought of
transcription haze my mental open eye?

The kindly search for growth, the gracious de-
sire to exist of the flowers, my near ecstasy at existing
among them

The privilege to witness my existence—you too
must seek the sun . . .

My books piled up before me for my use

waiting in space where I placed them, they
haven't disappeared, time's left its remnants and qual-
ities for me to use—my words piled up, my texts, my
manuscripts, my loves.

I had a moment of clarity, saw the feeling in
the heart of things, walked out to the garden crying.

Saw the red blossoms in the night light, sun's
gone, they had all grown, in a moment, and were waiting stopped in time for the day sun to come and give
them. . . .

Flowers which as in a dream at sunset I watered
faithfully not knowing how much I loved them.

I am so lonely in my glory—except they too out
there—I looked up—those red bush blossoms beckon-
ing and peering in the window waiting in blind love,
their leaves too have hope and are upturned top flat
to the sky to receive—all creation open to receive—the
flat earth itself.

The music descends, as does the tall bending stalk of the heavy blossom, because it has to, to stay alive, to continue to the last drop of joy.

The world knows the love that's in its breast as in the flower, the suffering lonely world.

The Father is merciful.

The light socket is crudely attached to the ceiling, after the house was built, to receive a plug which sticks in it alright, and serves my phonograph now . . .

The closet door is open for me, where I left it, since I left it open, it has graciously stayed open.

The kitchen has no door, the hole there will admit me should I wish to enter the kitchen.

I remember when I first got laid, H.P. graciously took my cherry, I sat on the docks of Provincetown, age 23, joyful, elevated in hope with the Father, the door to the womb was open to admit me if I wished to enter.

There are unused electricity plugs all over my house if I ever need them.

The kitchen window is open, to admit air . . .

The telephone—sad to relate—sits on the floor—I haven't the money to get it connected—

I want people to bow as they see me and say he is gifted with poetry, he has seen the presence of the Creator.

And the Creator gave me a shot of his presence to gratify my wish, so as not to cheat me of my yearning for him.

Berkeley, September 8, 1955

SUNFLOWER SUTRA

I walked on the banks of the tincan banana dock and
    sat down under the huge shade of a Southern
    Pacific locomotive to look at the sunset over the
    box house hills and cry.

Jack Kerouac sat beside me on a busted rusty iron
    pole, companion, we thought the same thoughts
    of the soul, bleak and blue and sad-eyed, sur-
    rounded by the gnarled steel roots of trees of
    machinery.

The oily water on the river mirrored the red sky, sun
    sank on top of final Frisco peaks, no fish in that
    stream, no hermit in those mounts, just our-
    selves rheumy-eyed and hungover like old bums
    on the riverbank, tired and wily.

Look at the Sunflower, he said, there was a dead gray
    shadow against the sky, big as a man, sitting
    dry on top of a pile of ancient sawdust—

—I rushed up enchanted—it was my first sunflower,
    memories of Blake—my visions—Harlem

and Hells of the Eastern rivers, bridges clanking Joes
    Greasy Sandwiches, dead baby carriages, black
    treadless tires forgotten and unretreaded, the
    poem of the riverbank, condoms & pots, steel

[handwritten margin note:] vision of William Blake in apartment (some claim relation to "free love" movement)

knives, nothing stainless, only the dank muck
and the razor-sharp artifacts passing into the
past—

So, this beautiful, natural thing has been blackened by the soot of the city, of industrialism

and the gray Sunflower poised against the sunset,
crackly bleak and dusty with the smut and smog
and smoke of olden locomotives in its eye—
corolla of bleary spikes pushed down and broken like
a battered crown, seeds fallen out of its face,
soon-to-be-toothless mouth of sunny air, sun-
rays obliterated on its hairy head like a dried
wire spiderweb,

leaves stuck out like arms out of the stem, gestures
from the sawdust root, broke pieces of plaster
fallen out of the black twigs, a dead fly in its ear,

Unholy battered old thing you were, my sunflower O
my soul, I loved you then!

The grime was no man's grime but death and human
locomotives,

he is personifying the grime as a "black" man

all that dress of dust, that veil of darkened railroad
skin, that smog of cheek, that eyelid of black
mis'ry, that sooty hand or phallus or protuber-
ance of artificial worse-than-dirt—industrial—
modern—all that civilization spotting your
crazy golden crown—

the petals

and those blear thoughts of death and dusty loveless
eyes and ends and withered roots below, in the

home-pile of sand and sawdust, rubber dollar
bills, skin of machinery, the guts and innards
of the weeping coughing car, the empty lonely
tincans with their rusty tongues alack, what
more could I name, the smoked ashes of some
cock cigar, the cunts of wheelbarrows and the
milky breasts of cars, wornout asses out of chairs
& sphincters of dynamos—all these
entangled in your mummied roots—and you there
standing before me in the sunset, all your glory
in your form!
A perfect beauty of a sunflower! a perfect excellent
lovely sunflower existence! a sweet natural eye
to the new hip moon, woke up alive and excited
grasping in the sunset shadow sunrise golden
monthly breeze!
How many flies buzzed round you innocent of your
grime, while you cursed the heavens of the railroad and your flower soul?
Poor dead flower? when did you forget you were a
flower? when did you look at your skin and
decide you were an impotent dirty old locomotive? the ghost of a locomotive? the specter and
shade of a once powerful mad American locomotive?

You were never no locomotive, Sunflower, you were a
   sunflower!

And you Locomotive, you are a locomotive, forget me
   not!

So I grabbed up the skeleton thick sunflower and stuck
   it at my side like a scepter,

and deliver my sermon to my soul, and Jack's soul
   too, and anyone who'll listen,

—We're not our skin of grime, we're not our dread
   bleak dusty imageless locomotive, we're all
   beautiful golden sunflowers inside, we're bles-
   sed by our own seed & golden hairy naked ac-
   complishment-bodies growing into mad black
   formal sunflowers in the sunset, spied on by our
   eyes under the shadow of the mad locomotive
   riverbank sunset Frisco hilly tincan evening sit-
   down vision.

                                        Berkeley, 1955

AMERICA

America I've given you all and now I'm nothing.
America two dollars and twentyseven cents January
      17, 1956.
I can't stand my own mind.
America when will we end the human war?
Go fuck yourself with your atom bomb.
I don't feel good don't bother me.
I won't write my poem till I'm in my right mind.
America when will you be angelic?
When will you take off your clothes?
When will you look at yourself through the grave?
When will you be worthy of your million Trotskyites?
America why are your libraries full of tears?
America when will you send your eggs to India?
I'm sick of your insane demands.
When can I go into the supermarket and buy what I
      need with my good looks?
America after all it is you and I who are perfect not
      the next world.
Your machinery is too much for me.
You made me want to be a saint.
There must be some other way to settle this argument.
Burroughs is in Tangiers I don't think he'll come back
      it's sinister.

Are you being sinister or is this some form of practical
        joke?
I'm trying to come to the point.
I refuse to give up my obsession.
America stop pushing I know what I'm doing.
America the plum blossoms are falling.
I haven't read the newspapers for months, everyday
        somebody goes on trial for murder.
America I feel sentimental about the Wobblies.
America I used to be a communist when I was a kid
        I'm not sorry.
I smoke marijuana every chance I get.
I sit in my house for days on end and stare at the roses
        in the closet.
When I go to Chinatown I get drunk and never get laid.
My mind is made up there's going to be trouble.
You should have seen me reading Marx.
My psychoanalyst thinks I'm perfectly right.
I won't say the Lord's Prayer.
I have mystical visions and cosmic vibrations.
America I still haven't told you what you did to Uncle
        Max after he came over from Russia.

I'm addressing you.
Are you going to let your emotional life be run by
        Time Magazine?

I'm obsessed by Time Magazine.

I read it every week.

Its cover stares at me every time I slink past the corner
candystore.

I read it in the basement of the Berkeley Public Library.

It's always telling me about responsibility. Business-
men are serious. Movie producers are serious.
Everybody's serious but me. *(not serious?)*

It occurs to me that I am America. ←

I am talking to myself again.

Asia is rising against me.

I haven't got a chinaman's chance.

I'd better consider my national resources.

My national resources consist of two joints of
marijuana millions of genitals an unpublishable
private literature that goes 1400 miles an hour
and twenty-five-thousand mental institutions.

I say nothing about my prisons nor the millions of
underprivileged who live in my flowerpots
under the light of five hundred suns.

I have abolished the whorehouses of France, Tangiers
is the next to go.

My ambition is to be President despite the fact that
I'm a Catholic. *(Kennedy ran in '60 election)*

America how can I write a holy litany in your silly
    mood?

I will continue like Henry Ford my strophes are as
    individual as his automobiles more so they're
    all different sexes.

America I will sell you strophes $2500 apiece $500
    down on your old strophe

America free Tom Mooney

America save the Spanish Loyalists

America Sacco & Vanzetti must not die

America I am the Scottsboro boys.

America when I was seven momma took me to Com-
    munist Cell meetings they sold us garbanzos a
    handful per ticket a ticket costs a nickel and the
    speeches were free everybody was angelic and
    sentimental about the workers it was all so sin-
    cere you have no idea what a good thing the
    party was in 1835 Scott Nearing was a grand
    old man a real mensch Mother Bloor made me
    cry I once saw Israel Amter plain. Everybody
    must have been a spy.

America you don't really want to go to war.

America it's them bad Russians.

Them Russians them Russians and them Chinamen.
    And them Russians.

The Russia wants to eat us alive. The Russia's power
   mad. She wants to take our cars from out our
   garages. *exceptionalist*
Her wants to grab Chicago. Her needs a Red *Readers'*
   Digest. Her wants our auto plants in Siberia.
   Him big bureaucracy running our fillingsta-
   tions.
That no good. Ugh. Him make Indians learn read.
   Him need big black niggers. Hah. Her make us
   all work sixteen hours a day. Help.
America this is quite serious.
America this is the impression I get from looking in
   the television set.
America is this correct?
I'd better get right down to the job. → *writing*
It's true I don't want to join the Army or turn lathes
   in precision parts factories, I'm nearsighted and
   psychopathic anyway.
America I'm putting my queer shoulder to the wheel.

Berkeley, January 17, 1956

— though marginalized, he matters and
belongs to America

IN THE BAGGAGE ROOM
AT GREYHOUND

I

In the depths of the Greyhound Terminal
sitting dumbly on a baggage truck looking at the sky
      waiting for the Los Angeles Express to depart
worrying about eternity over the Post Office roof in
      the night-time red downtown heaven,
staring through my eyeglasses I realized shuddering
      these thoughts were not eternity, nor the poverty
      of our lives, irritable baggage clerks,
nor the millions of weeping relatives surrounding the
      buses waving goodbye,
nor other millions of the poor rushing around from
      city to city to see their loved ones,
nor an indian dead with fright talking to a huge cop
      by the Coke machine,
nor this trembling old lady with a cane taking the last
      trip of her life,
nor the red-capped cynical porter collecting his quar-
      ters and smiling over the smashed baggage,
nor me looking around at the horrible dream,
nor mustached negro Operating Clerk named Spade,
      dealing out with his marvelous long hand the
      fate of thousands of express packages,

nor fairy Sam in the basement limping from leaden
        trunk to trunk,

nor Joe at the counter with his nervous breakdown
        smiling cowardly at the customers,

nor the grayish-green whale's stomach interior loft
        where we keep the baggage in hideous racks,

hundreds of suitcases full of tragedy rocking back and
        forth waiting to be opened,

nor the baggage that's lost, nor damaged handles,
        nameplates vanished, busted wires & broken
        ropes, whole trunks exploding on the concrete
        floor,

nor seabags emptied into the night in the final
        warehouse.

II

Yet Spade reminded me of Angel, unloading a bus,

dressed in blue overalls black face official Angel's work-
        man cap,

pushing with his belly a huge tin horse piled high with
        black baggage,

looking up as he passed the yellow light bulb of the loft

and holding high on his arm an iron shepherd's crook.

III

It was the racks, I realized, sitting myself on top of
them now as is my wont at lunchtime to rest
my tired foot,

it was the racks, great wooden shelves and stanchions
posts and beams assembled floor to roof jumbled
with baggage,

—the Japanese white metal postwar trunk gaudily
flowered & headed for Fort Bragg,

one Mexican green paper package in purple rope
adorned with names for Nogales,

hundreds of radiators all at once for Eureka,

crates of Hawaiian underwear,

rolls of posters scattered over the Peninsula, nuts to
Sacramento,

one human eye for Napa,

an aluminum box of human blood for Stockton

and a little red package of teeth for Calistoga—

it was the racks and these on the racks I saw naked
in electric light the night before I quit,

the racks were created to hang our possessions, to keep
us together, a temporary shift in space,

God's only way of building the rickety structure of
Time,

to hold the bags to send on the roads, to carry our
luggage from place to place
looking for a bus to ride us back home to Eternity
where the heart was left and farewell tears
began.

IV

A swarm of baggage sitting by the counter as the trans-
continental bus pulls in.
The clock registering 12:15 A.M., May 9, 1956, the
second hand moving forward, red.
Getting ready to load my last bus.—Farewell, Walnut
Creek Richmond Vallejo Portland Pacific
Highway
Fleet-footed Quicksilver, God of transience.
One last package sits lone at midnight sticking up out
of the Coast rack high as the dusty fluorescent
light.

The wage they pay us is too low to live on. Tragedy
reduced to numbers.
This for the poor shepherds. I am a communist.

Farewell ye Greyhound where I suffered so much,
    hurt my knee and scraped my hand and built
    my pectoral muscles big as vagina.

May 9, 1956

looks out of the heart
  burning with purity—
for the burden of life
  is love,

but we carry the weight
  wearily,
and so must rest
in the arms of love
  at last,
must rest in the arms
  of love.

No rest
  without love,
no sleep
  without dreams
of love—
  be mad or chill
obsessed with angels
  or machines,
the final wish
  is love
—cannot be bitter,
  cannot deny,

cannot withhold
        if denied:

the weight is too heavy

            —must give
for no return
            as thought
is given
            in solitude
in all the excellence
            of its excess.

The warm bodies
            shine together
in the darkness,
            the hand moves
to the center
            of the flesh,
the skin trembles
            in happiness
and the soul comes
            joyful to the eye—

yes, yes,
            that's what

I wanted,
     I always wanted,
I always wanted,
     to return
to the body
     where I was born.

San Jose, 1954

WILD ORPHAN

Blandly mother
takes him strolling
        by railroad and by river
—he's the son of the absconded
        hot rod angel—
and he imagines cars
        and rides them in his dreams,

so lonely growing up among
        the imaginary automobiles
and dead souls of Tarrytown

        to create
out of his own imagination
        the beauty of his wild
forebears—a mythology
        he cannot inherit.

Will he later hallucinate
        his gods? Waking
among mysteries with
        an insane gleam
of recollection?

The recognition—
something so rare
in his soul,
met only in dreams
—nostalgias
of another life.

A question of the soul.
And the injured
losing their injury
in their innocence
—a cock, a cross,
an excellence of love.

And the father grieves
in flophouse
complexities of memory
a thousand miles
away, unknowing
of the unexpected
youthful stranger
bumming toward his door.

New York, April 13, 1952

In back of the real

railroad yard in San Jose
　　　I wandered desolate
in front of a tank factory
　　　and sat on a bench
near the switchman's shack.

A flower lay on the hay on
　　　the asphalt highway
—the dread hay flower
　　　I thought—It had a
brittle black stem and
　　　corolla of yellowish dirty
spikes like Jesus' inchlong
　　　crown, and a soiled
dry center cotton tuft
　　　like a used shaving brush
that's been lying under
　　　the garage for a year.

Yellow, yellow flower, and
　　　flower of industry,
tough spiky ugly flower,
　　　flower nonetheless,

with the form of the great yellow
Rose in your brain!
This is the flower of the World.

San Jose, 1954

ALSO BY ALLEN GINSBERG

Pocket Poets Series

Kaddish and Other Poems

Reality Sandwiches

Planet News

The Fall of America: Poems of These States

Mind Breaths

Plutonian Ode and Other Poems

The Yage Letters Redux (with William S. Burroughs)

Travels with Ginsberg, A Postcard Book

Composed on the Tongue:
A Book of Literary Conversations

Anthologies, Interviews, Essays, Bibliographies

The New American Poetry 1945-1960. (D. Allen, ed.), Grove Press, 1960.

A Casebook of the Beat (T. Parkinson, ed.), Thomas Y. Crowell, 1961.

Paris Review Interviews (w/Tom Clark), Viking, 1967.

The Poem in Its Skin (P. Carroll, ed.) Big Table/Follett, 1968.

Playboy. (interview w/P. Carroll), 1969.

Scenes Along the Road. (Photos) (A. Charters, ed.), Gotham Book Mart, 1970.

Bibliography of the Works of Allen Ginsberg 1943-1967. (G. Dowden, ed.),City Lights Books, 1971.

Poetics of the New American Poetry. (D. Allen & W. Tallman, eds.), Grove, 1973.

The Beat Book, 1974; and *The Beat Diary,* 1977. (A. K. & G. Knight, eds.)

Loka: Journal of Naropa Institute. Anchor Doubleday, vol. 1-1975, vol. 2-1976.

The New Naked Poetry. (Berg & Mezey, eds.), Bobbs-Merrill, 1976.

Phonograph Records

Howl and Other Poems. Fantasy-Galaxy Records #7013, Berkeley, 1959.

Kaddish. Atlantic Verbum Series 4001, 1966. (op)

Wm. Blake's Songs of Innocence & of Experience tuned by A.G., MGM/Verve, 1970 (op)

Blake Album II. Fantasy-Galaxy Records, 1971 (unissued)

First Blues. John Hammond Sr., Producer (unissued)